Be My Reader

Be My Reader

Alec Finlay

Shearsman Books

First published in the United Kingdom in 2012 by
Shearsman Books
50 Westons Hill Drive
Emersons Green
Bristol
BS16 7DF

Shearsman Books Ltd Registered Office
30–31 St. James Place, Mangotsfield, Bristol BS16 9JB
(this address not for correspondence)

www.shearsman.com

ISBN 978-1-84861-107-8

Acknowledgements
The author would like to thank those editors and publishers who have
featured some of these poems in journals, magazines, anthologies
and books, including *Says You* (Oystercatcher Press, 2009),
island magazine 15, and *Sunfish Magazine* 5.

'The Sunken Bell (Dunwich)': composed for Waterlog
(commissioned by Film and Video Umbrella, 2007).
'family' & 'New Model Glider': first published *Question your teaspoons*
(Calder Wood Press, 2012).
'The Wittgenstein House (Skjolden)': first published *Ludwig
Wittgenstein: There Where You Are Not*, with Michael Nedo &
Guy Moreton (Black Dog Publishing, 2005).
'dance trace' was first realised as an animation
(commissioned by Dance City, Newcastle, 2006).
'I Know a Poem': first published West House Books, 2004.

Contents

Be My Reader

The Wittgenstein House (Skjolden)

*Something really does happen to most people who go into
the north—they become at least aware of the creative
opportunity which the physical fact of the country
represents and ... come to measure their own work and life
against that rather staggering creative possibility—they
become, in effect, philosophers.*

— Glenn Gould

•

Russell said it would be dark.
Wittgenstein said he hated daylight.

Russell said it would be lonely.
Wittgenstein said he prostituted his mind
talking to intelligent people.

Russell said he was mad.
Wittgenstein said God preserve him from sanity.

There's the sign across the lake

The famous Austrian philosopher Ludwig Wittgenstein (1889–1951) owned in 1914 a hut here in Skjolden. The foundations of this hut you can see on the other side of Eidsvatnet. Wittgenstein worked there with the manuscripts of the Tractatus *and of the* Philosophical Investigations.

I went back to Skjolden
and the dark circle
of mountains

to look for my own place
in the glen
of a shadowed world

where what I find
is shown in
how I think and live.

In the north day
gives way to night
slowly evening

stretches for miles
through a landscape
suffused with light.

The clouded Fjell peaks
are gone again
into white lift.

There is seeing, there is rain,
a smirr slowly
gives way to sun.

At Vasbakken the water-
fall gleams whitely
in the dark.

What I forget each time
is how the rush of falls
fills the valley,

as just under my window
the burn clinks
softly away.

Luster fjord is black
lake blue river
eddies copper-green.

The damp makes me
rheumy, glandy
eyes gone bleary

with my nose sunk
in tea tree and some
sun my only remedy.

The human body
is the best picture
of the human soul.

Make your way past
the wooden sign
  WITTGENSTEIN

Along the lane wild rasps
& nettles line the verges,
  puddles fill the track.

All the small fields meet up
in corners, each with its
  own suitable barn—

stone huts, wood shacks
or corrugated iron lean-tos;
  stacks of felled thinnings

like pencils in a box
and neat xylotheques
  of peeling birch logs.

Now step into the wood
through willowherb, elder,
  rowan & birch.

The path walks up
through Guy's arch
  of bending branches,

then down beside the lake—
take care over slippy rocks,
  ferns & brambles.

You'll see the walled harbour
where his row boat anchored.
    Follow the spray-marked 'W's

on the two scarred findlings
that seem to be resting on
    each other's shoulders.

To your right are still tides
of scree winter washed
   down the slope

splashed with grey & orange lichen.
Then, when the trees get too thick,
   turn and zig-zag

up the steep path.
The metal hoops
   of Wittgenstein's pulley

are still fastened to the cliff –
the rig at the foot stolen
   for some professor's trophy.

Here, on the plateau, perched
above the lake, the foundations
   are a man-made rock.

Stand where the verandah was
& lock out over
   the grey curtain of mountains

their rippling reflections.
See the view that W chose:
   a landscape utterly simple.

the sky   is so high   clouds pass

gentle breath   rises   from the lake

huffs of white stratus   gather low

in the valley   flexuous weather

nebulous shapes   form & fall

draw up   sheer cliffs   to sky

touch stone   plumes ravel   unravel

in the space   between

droplets
on
branches
&
soft
mosses
&
along
the
tears
of
the
spiders'
webs
my
boots
brush
back
to
water

The immediate is a stream

In my childhood kitchen
Norway was the dark cast jotul
graven with a Godly inscription.

Two woodsmen with a band-saw
bend to the pine's trunk.
There are bears in this forest.

Now in the fjord valleys
orchards are decked
with red Sogn apples.

Bolstad promised Ludwig
a crate for Christmas 1939
if the import duty wasn't too steep.

And though it's only
the third week of August
the rowans are ripe.

I fill a plastic bag
of berries for jelly,
boil the juice in a pan

and bring back a thermos
full with just enough
to set these two jars.

I would like to set out my life clearly,
to have it plainly in front of me,
to survey all of the connections.

The wanderer is still searching
for a place from which to look,
a place in which to think.

Hochreith
the hunting lodge on the family estate.

Whewells Court (K10)
Moore's old room with the view
over the rooftops.

Trachenburg
in the mountains,
the teacher's little room
with its wooden table.

Das Rathaus, Olmütz
leave from the front spent with Engelmann,
the high tower of the city hall
with its magnificent view.

Hütteldorf Monastery, Klosterneuburg
the gardener's hut
beside the graveyard.

Kundmangasse
LW, architect for his sister Margaret's house,
designed every window-lock and door,

an exposition of functional perfection.
It was, said Hermine, *too perfect to live in.*

Rosroe
The last pool of darkness
at the edge of Europe.

Like Skjolden, the cottage looks to the west,
protected by a ring of mountains.
Killary fjord ebbs to the Atlantic,
Sogne to the Nordsjøen.

Skjolden
Always there was Skjolden.

I can't imagine that I could have worked anywhere
as I do here.
It's the quiet and, perhaps,
the wonderful scenery;
I mean its quiet seriousness.

There it seems to me that
I gave birth to new paths
of thought within me.
There I had some thoughts of my own.

I have built my house away from anyone.
I long to see a human face in the morning.

One day at lunch in the kitchen Tommy Mullerkins pointed to the table and said, "I seen a robin coming in and eating off this table. Your man was like St. Francis with the birds on his shoulders and his hands. He was so keen to watch sea birds that he asked me to build him a hut on Inishbarna."

"Did you do this?"

"No, because, you see, if I'd built him a hut on the island, he'd have wanted me to be carrying down the curragh on my back to the shore and rowing him out there every day. We might have been caught in a storm. He asked would I let him sleep in my house, but I said no. There was only my bed he could have slept in ... When he was leaving he gave me some money to buy food for the birds in the garden."

"Did you do this?"

"Not for long. He had those birds so tame that the cats ate them.

—Richard Murphy's diary

Those friends Wittgenstein
cared for most
visited him at Skjolden.

   David Pinsent
   Hermann Hänsel
   Ludwig Hänsel
   Arvid Sjögren
   Gilbert Pattisson
   Marguerite Respinger
   Francis Skinner
   Ben Richards

When the *sorge* became more
than he could bear—

when there was no letter
from David or Francis,

when he went to be alone
and was only lonely—

then the porcupine would
climb the path to Eide Farm

& visit his wiry friend
the teacher, Anna Rebni.

As a gift he had a new ladle
made for her well.

When she demurred
he took hold the old one

and flung it away
into the fields.

Ibsen's Brand came from
among these mountains.

a light in the night sky

a star fades

set in dark cliffs

the light of a hut

I ought to have become a star in the sky.
Instead of which I remain stuck on the earth
and now I am slowly fading.

24

If I am unable to grasp
the mechanism
of thought

then from this view
I can still learn
how to see.

The foundations
are a razed
platform.

Two white birch
grow from
the open cellar.

*Somehow, I must find
my way out
of this forest.*

*LW, Skjolden i Sogni
1913–14, 1921, 1931, 1936–37, 1950*

AF, Skjolden i Sogni
August 2001, 2002

The Sunken Bell (Dunwich)

for Guy Moreton

walk the shingle's
sea worn stones
salted pebbles

you'll find amber
or a heart

like the ones Gerhard
found before us

he was more discerning
about their shapes

over the road the sea
under the waves
the beach

this morning the field floats
swans on a flood
of reflected light

where later
out my window
a second moon shimmers

whatever changes the sea
holds the sky's colour

stars are clear to steer or
swim or drown under

the waves wake
the sea's dream

at All Saints the last grave
faces the cliff's edge

   St Bartholomew's
   St Michael's
   St Anthony's
   St Leonard's
   St Nicholas'
   St Martin's
   St Katherine's
   St Peter's
   Blackfriars
   St John the Baptist

all sunk: they say
you can hear their bells
toll in the swell
of a high tide

let's cast a new bell
from molten flame

sink it deep
before the sea
covers the land again

Some Island Views

for Gerry Loose

the taxi driver
tells it this way:
if a life was broken
into little pieces
and thrown up in the air
and landed on the islands
it would not be
such a bad life
after all.

•

the island
tells it this way:
if a taxi driver was
thrown up in the air
after a such bad life
and landed
on little islands
after all it would not
be broken into.

•

after all
the not landed islands
were broken
on the air
and thrown up into
such bad little pieces

the taxi driver
tells it this way:
be a life.

•

after the island
the little landed
and thrown up into
bad taxi driver
tells it this way:
in such pieces
life would not
be all broken
on the air.

•

afterlife
tells it this way:
if the taxi driver
be all broken
and such landed
into the bad air
it would not be
thrown up on
the little islands.

Croisset

for Ian Stephen & The Captains

Some sailor or other
taking a bearing
by the light

of Flaubert's lamp
as he writes
deep into the night.

If You Ask an Orkney Fireman What He Does When There Is a Fire on Hoy This Is What He Will Say

Wait for the ferry

(for Andrew & Neil)

Cove (Kilcreggan)

Known cures for melancholy

    a purple thistle without prickles
    cloud shadows stroking the hills

    the rain finding a new angle
    leaving drops like tiny teeth
            set beneath the rail

    a faint path winding
    through each sea meadow

    the police launch observing
    the peace camp
    all day and all night long

    l'amour en Ecosse en plein air
    love on a blanket under a jacket
    avec moon, stars, kisses & midges

New Model Glider

for Ailie

Her nose a black bruise
of plasticine Dad launches

up she dips in cupped arcs
hiccuping over thistles and molehills.

We watch her fly and wish
for a wee thermal

to scoop her magically
to the road or

even more wonderful
a disaster in the peaty burn.

As the elastic band whirrs
unwound I run after

chasing the tail in my wellies
arms out to catch her

the moment before
she touches down on the turf

my ankles tumble over.
Smash goes the balsa.

The Scottish Question

for Zoë

If you need an answer
then the answer's no.

•

The Scottish app

i-dears

In the Land of Brodie

The rolls of all the world
are not for me—
for my part I want only
the little white rolls of Scotland
that are dry and taste of nothing
and break the heart.

•

I'm going to write you
a wee note

and say the nice things
you don't say to people's faces.

A Missing iPhone

After the Gaelic Translations of Alexander Carmichael, from Carmina Gadelica

Na ho I eadh ho ho ill a bhi,
Na ho ibh o ha o ri ho a ro,
No ho hao ri o bho learthag

I lost my lovely iPhone
  On Friday just gone

It was no bigger than a Kitkat
  And it was better than a Wii

It fell among the bracken
  And I have not found it yet

I'm bored of looking for it
  At the bottom of the hill

I wouldn't loan it to anyone
  Not even my sister

Or to Big Eck
  Even if he asked, he wouldn't get it.

Na ho I eadh ho ho ill a bhi,
Na ho ibh o ha o ri ho a ro,
No ho hao ri o bho learthag

Mortimer's Logic (Rosroe)

for David Connearn

The EU pay us now
not to cut the peat
but I won't take the money
for what would happen
if I got used to it
and then they decided
to take it back?

Lucy's Italia

Actually Totti's a fool.
And he's got a horrid mouth.

It's Canavarro's hair
that I'm worried about;

it used to be pudding–
bowl shaped and glossy.

The main highlight
for me is when they

bring on my *vero amore*
Alessandro Del Piero

towards the end
of each game—

I just flutter
into butter.

The Wait

I rock the swing-seat to-and-fro
  in the low sun
    chatting with Christine

comparing lives,
  enjoying the feeling
    you're somewhere here

but out of sight,
  knowing soon
    you will reappear

it's us who will be
  leaving together.
    Upstairs

with the girls
  kneeling on soft cushions
    surrounded by scarves,

feathers and colours
  you help Grace
    out of or into

her blue mermaid dress
  gluing sparkles
    under your eyes.

Christine smiles and says,
  'they didn't get it from me',
    Ross picks out a tune

on a musical toy;
  in this home
    where each room

is a child's, each an artist's.
  Now it's gone dark,
    the others have left

and I'm alone
  gently swinging
    waiting for you

 to come down
  the turning stairs
    from your painted room.

L'Atalante

for Holly

Where three rivers meet
we enter the water
feel the flow pull our limbs.

Still in the trees
there is birdsong
the evening light forgives.

I watch your shadow
as you sleep
go out in the intense dawn

that you may know me
in the sun
for the time i'm gone.

We come together shuddering
your fingers clutching
at an ear of wheat.

Thought's thorn turns
the point in.

What's fallen from me
lies at my feet.

You say sorrel?
I want to hear sorrow
hear your sadness heal
but you're alone.

Yesterday I swam in The Medwin
looking for your face
smiling back at me
from under the water.

In visage a wraith's beautiful
but has no tongue.

your love is a clifftop from which I cannot f-

family

father
is the war of all things

mother's
word is ward

family
is a shipwreck

children
are the revolution

Glad Gold

Glenn Gould's Goldberg Variations (Variations)

Since you asked
  there was an alluvial
   this morning
the leavings of
  the storm—
   red winter berries
shiny & wind blown
  in the cracks of the paving
   and in the gutter
markings of wind
  & of rain.

•

Glenn Gould, hmmm ...
  you said
   and I haven't told you
about that piece yet—
  a notation of the hums
   on Gould's *Goldberg Variations*—
the voice preserved
  on magnetic tape
   transcribed as a score
performed on a Steinway
   (model 317)
    cello (solo)
voice (solo)
  and choir.

•

The *Goldberg* is *nacht music*
  aria & variations—
    little songs without words
played to put
  a King
    to sleep.

•

Gould's performance
  announced a figure
    of artistic genius—
the hums his variations
  on the *Variations*
    a habit
learned from mother
  his first teacher.

I apologise for
  singing along
    but I would play
less well
  without it ...
    and for my gestures
– semaphore for sidemen –
  a desire to externalise
    not the music
or even my own
  relation to it
    but perhaps
the responsibility
  for it.

∙

This new score
  gives the listeners ears
    for the barely audible
the alluvials
  that we might call
    faith & failure
gift & wound
  glad & gold.

Goldberg Variations, BWV 988; J. S. Bach (1742)
Glenn Gould (1955)

Three Composers

Xenia & John

After her
marriage

the conductor's
wife

took up
percussion.

Arnold

Schoenberg composed
his first Sonata

after he received Vol. 'S'
of *The Encyclopedia.*

Frédéric

play like velvet
practice in the dark

peeking under the chairs
the mice are all ears
as they listen to the music
it soothes their fears

during the *mazurka*
one mouse whispers
to the other mouse
shall we dance?

telyn

for Rhodri Davies

grace

      bends

                  the neck

          a bow of

RAMONA

RAMONES TRIBUTE BAND

REQUIRE
DRUMMER

ESSENTIAL REQUIREMENTS

PACE
STAMINA
ENTHUSIASM

INTERESTED ?

As the Sailor Said to the Mermaid

for Alex

How less beautiful
is that

now that it's
not wet?

On Enquiring How a Friend's Gift
Had Been Received

for Rob

The knickers
went down
very nicely.

Lauraisms

for Imp

the singer had
a distinctive vice

•

the world
was her lobster

•

he was as bald
as a badger

Knit (1)

I have not
developed

my own
patterns

yet.
I am still

learning.
But when

I do
I promise

that
I will

show them
to you.

Knit (2)

for Goose

It's best to knit after dark
when the sheep are asleep.

(Thomas Holmes Mason, *The Island of Ireland, 1936)*

54

Sew

stitches
hold

where
they're
hidden

Bound

for Rachel Bollen

I have just very simply
stitched them

but I think the thread
is probably perfection.

SAE

We hope for your understanding
when we must tell you

that this book is too special
for our publishing program.

typing

typing within reason
typing furiously
typing on tiptoe
typing touching
typing A,B,C
typing R.S.I.
untyping

MORI

The pollsters claim:
our polls

are more accurate
than the vote.

(Her from Grantham)

Then the lucozade
lights went on

in the back
of her eyes.

Conway Hall

The old Socialist
insists that his Socialists

are chalk and cheese
to the other Socialists.

(Chalk and cheese
isn't strong enough.)

The Prime Minister
has given us his word

This is going to be
the *best* worst time
that we've *ever* had.

Banks

Their assets
are pretty vanilla.

They stick
to their knitting.

Their figures
have all

but dropped
off the edge.

It's time they
had a haircut.

St Matthew (Revised Version)

God's
on the side
of The Householder.

says you

the pundit poems

David Begg says

Artur Boruc's
made a kipper
out of that

•

Steve Claridge says

this fellow
Alberto Riera's
the full McCoy

•

Steve Stone says

the winger's
running round like
he's broken his leg

•

Kevin Gallagher says

the right-back
is inillegible
for this cup tie

•

Alan Shearer says

he got them off
to a good start
with a great finish

•

Robbie Savage says

he's gone through
that defence
like butter

•

The commentators share a giggle over

Ronaldo's speedy legover

More Fitba Poems

Chick speirs Wee Jinky

Jinky, when did ye ken
yer leg wiz broken?

When I seen Big Greigy
comin over tae tackle me

•

these days
football is just
so much gossip

•

I always
fall asleep

in-between
the goals

Archie Macpherson, in a radio football commentary Scotland v. Chile (late 1970s)

Ho! – did you see that!

R C A E N L G T E I R C S

football yarns

passed

woven

threaded

needled

jabbed

stabbed

dance trace

the	the
moment	moment
their	their
feet	feet
touch	touch
the	the
floor	floor
a	a
dance	dance
is	is
traced	traced
as	as
their	their
shadows	shadows
enter	enter
together	together

she	he
follows	leads
bends	lifts
her	his
knees	arms
and	and
points	stretches
her	his
toes	hands
and	open
her	reaches
fingers	up
while	while
their	their
heels	toes
brush	brush

the	the
boards	boards
now	now
she	he
is	turns
turning	her
slowly	slowly
around	around
touch	their
then	bodies
she	and
curves	he
low	arches
down	his
now	back
up	lifts

```
and            and
then           then


they           they
  fall         fall


other          following
   in          each


and            of
out            time
```

Cable

trunks shape dark shafts, everything wants more sun
after the rain it keeps on raining under the trees

the taste of wet brambles is pure, then they rot
everything grows with its roots in decay

there will be a reason leaves are curved but their veins run straight
the ash only becomes an ash up there, where it touches the clouds

there are paths made for us and paths we make alone
no two branches grow the same

everybody is waiting for somebody
equality is balancing different things

the sky is a mirror
we don't always know what we feel

the moon, void of light, reflects the sun
I need the scar to show

the butterflies are out flying their eyes
all attributes distinguish an order

an open hard cradles emptiness
islands are islands because stone withstands sea

our lives are so different, your house is cold, mine is warm
the brighter the leaves the more pain the tree feels

Day For Night

We mark the trees
  for felling
    with two flashes

•

A cure for sap
  finger
    the dirt

•

A family fortune
  made trading
    in lichen

•

Shh! the mice
  are hiding
    their tails

Night For Day

for Caitlin DeSilvey

Light flung
  after dark
    dims the day

•

Wind through
  branches becomes
    the silences

•

Know your track
  how to find your way
    in the dark

•

In every path
  there is
    a fork

Hid in a Tale: a Folio of Leaves

for Ken Cockburn

Mile after mile
  dale after dale
    the lea flows, rolls

towards me. I take
  the stile afoot and step
    into the screen

of branches. Clustered
  azalea fills my eyes;
    the young heather

springs gentle,
  affords me cover.
    Let's kindle a fire,

riffle affectionately
  and don a smile,
    after all's done.

Meanwhile a fog's
  fallen over the vale,
    a familiar fear

sinks over me.
  The oak's great bole
    affirms a reckoning.

Tree, hear my plea:
  forgive me; console
    a friend, so pale,

afraid; allow me
  to amble afternoon &
    evening, seeking meaning

in the whole affair.
  My sole afterthought:
    is this sorry tale

a figment or fable
  aflame in my mind?
    Let the breezes fondle

a familiar who played
  his role, a form of
    dissemble, a foolish

shadow-play; for guile
  afforded me no comfort.
    Now I leave this

dear green wood
  & in turning I turn
    over this new leaf.

leaf, embedded 25 times

E–D–W–I–N–M–O–R–G–A–N

pErjink barD, Whose brIghtness shiNes,
diMmer nOw; youR aGe An eoN

redEfining scotlanD's Weeness wIth soNnets,
Mercurial visitOrs, hoRsiemen, starlinGs And chaffiNches,

strangE Dialects tWinned wIth toNgues
froM hOme, woRld lanGuages mAking frieNds;

dEftly benDing Words Into infiNite
forMs, cOnstructions foR holdinG And loviNg,

poEms openeD With happIness, penNing
anagraMs Of youR orGan And hymeN,

sharEd iDeograms Within whIch Nothing
becoMes pOetry: foR nothinG sAys somethiNg,

dEsires worDs Which staIn, iNking Memories,
retOuching pResbyterian Grey, reveAling raiNbows,

mEanings transmittedD With tIme's passiNg—
instaMatics, space-pOems, computeR-greetings, video-
boxinG, orAcular techNician—

thosE Dipped straWberries stIll shiNe,
reMembered Over-and-oveR. Given deAth kNots

lifE's enD, We persIst iN reMembering
pOems aRe messaGes, trAnsmitting oN-and-on-and-on-

(i.m. Yeddie)

I Know a Poem

for Thomas Evans

I KNOW A MAN
I KNOW A MAN
I KNOW A MAN
I know
a man

As I said
as I sd to my
As I sd, to my friend
as I sd to my friend John
As I sd to my friend John
john
i sd
So I said to my friend John
… John, I sd
to my friend John be-
friend, because I am
because I am always
always talking, John
cause I am always talking,
John, I said, the
talking, John I sd
I sd, which was not
(which was not his name)
which is not his name
which was not his real name
his name, the darkness
the darkness surrounds us,
this darkness
the darkness surrounds us

the dark
ness
surrounds us, what
darkness sur-
rounds us, caught
surrounds us what
surrounds us
in the headlights, what
can we do
against it so
can we do against
what can we do against it
it, or else, shall we,
or else, shall we
& why not,
& why not
and why not buy
why not buy a
buy a goddamn
why not get a goddamn
goddam big car and
big car &
buy a goddamn big car—
big car,
a goddam big car
let's get a goddammed big car and

drive
drive he sd,
drive, he sd
drive, he said—
Drive the car

who drive
Drive he said
he sd &
he sd
Drive, he said, for
Christ's sake, and
for christ's sake
for chrissake watch
for christ's sake
for christ's sake
watch out
and just watch where you're going
where yr. going
look out where yr going
look out where you're going
look out where yr going.
where yr going
look out
where yr
going

(after Robert Creeley, 'I Know A Man')

Prayer

what the night shall bring
the day shall heal

what the day shall bring
the night shall heal

Epitaph

each of us
brushed by pollen

written in
dust

Notes

'The Wittgenstein House (Skjolden)': the original impetus for this poem was Ray Monk's biography, *Ludwig Wittgenstein: The Duty of Genius* (Penguin, 1991).

Richard Murphy's diary: *The Kick* (London: Granta, 2002).

Xenia & John: Xenia Cage (née Xenia Andreyevna Kashevaroff) was married to the American composer and poet John Cage.

'More Fitba Poems': *Chick*, as in Young; *Jinky*, as in Jimmy Johnstone; *Big Greigy*, as in John Greig.

Archie MacPherson: ancient relic of Scottish football commentators.

'Day For Night': *the mice are hiding their tails*, American folk-saying describing pinecones.

'Hid in a Tale: a Folio of Leaves': composed to celebrate Scottish Poetry Library: XXV.

'I Know a Poem': after Robert Creeley's 'I Know a Man'; and composed from the memories of Bob Arnold, David Connearn, Thomas Evans, Harry Gilonis, Kenny Goldsmith, Andrew Schelling, Brian Kim Stefans, Tom Raworth.

www.ingramcontent.com/pod-product-compliance
Lightning Source LLC
Chambersburg PA
CBHW031928080426
42734CB00007B/604